TIM ALBERTA - BREAKTHROUGH SUCCESS

How a Journalist Became a Best-Selling Author and a Voice of His Generation

HOFFMAN HARRY

Copyright

Table Of Contents

Title Page

Copyright 1

Table Of Contents 2

Introduction 5

CHAPTER 1 9

Early Life And Background 9

CHAPTER 2 13

Rise To Journalism 13

CHAPTER 3 17

Reporting Approach And Lifestyle 17

CHAPTER 4 21

Notable Interviews And Coverage 21

CHAPTER 5 25

Personal Life And Relationships 25

CHAPTER 6 29

Challenges And Victories 29

CHAPTER 7 33

Influence And Impact 33

CHAPTER 8 36

Key Lessons 36

CHAPTER 9 38

Transformative Exercises............................... 38

CONCLUSION 44

INTRODUCTION

Tim Alberta is a notable personality in American political journalism, noted for his astute analysis and in-depth reporting on the inner workings of Washington, D.C. His work has been distinguished by a devotion to seeking the truth and presenting a fair view of the complicated world of politics. From his early days as a young reporter to his present place as one of the most regarded voices in political journalism, Tim Alberta has made substantial contributions to the industry and has acquired a reputation as a trustworthy and prominent critic.

Tim Alberta's path in journalism started in his native state of Michigan, where he grew up with a flair for storytelling and a great interest in current affairs. He improved his talents as a writer and reporter while studying at Michigan State University, where he received a degree in journalism. After graduation, he began a career in political reporting, working for numerous magazines and earning excellent experience covering municipal and state politics.

In 2014, Tim Alberta joined National Review as a senior editor, where he immediately earned a reputation for himself as a knowledgeable and insightful critic of conservative politics. His work was marked by its depth and complexity, allowing readers a thorough comprehension of the subjects at hand. Alberta's ability to compress complicated political happenings into simple and appealing tales set him out as an emerging star in the field of political journalism.

Alberta's career took a big turn in 2019 when he joined Politico as its top political reporter. In this post, he broadened his reach and power, offering readers rare insights into the inner workings of Capitol Hill and the White House.

His reporting on the Trump administration and its influence on American politics gained worldwide recognition, confirming his status as a major voice on the subject.

One of Alberta's most famous contributions to political journalism came in the shape of his book, "American Carnage: On the Front Lines of the Republican Civil War and the Rise of President Trump." Published in 2019, the book offers a thorough examination of the Republican Party's evolution in the age of Trump, building on Alberta's extensive research and interviews with major participants in the political environment. "American Carnage" attracted significant notice and critical praise, establishing Alberta's place as a prominent expert on the junction of politics and ideology.

In addition to his writing, Tim Alberta has also created a reputation for himself as a recognized pundit and analyst, routinely appearing on television and radio to give informed thoughts on current happenings. His ability to express complicated subjects with clarity and accuracy has made him a sought-after voice in the media environment, further magnifying his effect on public conversation.

Tim Alberta's contributions to politics and media are notable not just for their depth and insight but also for their continuing effect on the national discussion. Through his reporting, writing, and analysis, he has given readers and viewers a greater knowledge of the forces affecting American politics, helping to guide public conversation and define the national narrative.

As he continues to make his imprint on the world of political journalism, Tim Alberta is devoted to keeping the greatest standards of honesty and professionalism in his work. His passion for truth-seeking and his unshakable commitment to offering impartial and insightful analysis have positioned him as a prominent figure in the profession, garnering him the respect and admiration of colleagues and readers alike.

In an age defined by rapid change and turmoil in American politics, Tim Alberta's relentless devotion to quality and his remarkable ability to make sense of it all have secured his position as an important voice in the national discourse. His work stands as a tribute to the ongoing power of outstanding journalism and its potential to educate, enlighten, and encourage meaningful discourse. As he continues to negotiate the ever-evolving environment of political reporting, there is little question that Tim Alberta will be a powerful force in molding our knowledge of the forces influencing our nation's destiny.

CHAPTER 1

EARLY LIFE AND BACKGROUND

Tim Alberta was born and reared in the state of Michigan, where he acquired a profound respect for storytelling and a keen interest in current affairs from an early age. Growing up in a close-knit household, he was imbued with a strong work ethic and a sense of curiosity that would define his future career in journalism.

Tim's parents had a vital effect in defining his early interests and ideals. His father, a dedicated blue-collar worker, taught him the significance of endurance and drive.

Tim's mother, a committed housewife, nourished his passion for reading and promoted his academic endeavors.

Their unflinching support and mentoring would be important in Tim's road toward becoming a famous figure in American political journalism.

As a young kid, Tim Alberta exhibited a natural flair for writing and storytelling. He was an ardent reader, reading books on a broad variety of themes and immersing himself in the world of literature. His early exposure to the power of words and ideas would create the groundwork for his future career as a journalist and novelist.

Tim's love for current affairs and politics was clear from an early age. He enthusiastically followed local and national news, striving to grasp the complicated forces at play in the world around him. His intense curiosity and intellectual drive drove him to participate in heated disputes with family members and friends, improving his ability to explain his views and beliefs clearly and with conviction.

Tim's scholastic experience started at a local public school, where he excelled academically and displayed a natural flair for writing and communication. His tutors saw his talent early on, urging him to follow his interests and explore the world of media. Tim's early years were defined by a strong desire for learning and a genuine devotion to intellectual advancement.

Upon graduating from high school, Tim Alberta opted to extend his studies at Michigan State University, where he sought a degree in journalism. The institution presented him with a rich and varied academic atmosphere, enabling him to broaden his knowledge and polish his talents as a writer and reporter. Tim's stay at Michigan State University will be essential in establishing his future professional path and placing him on the track toward becoming a strong voice in political journalism.

During his undergraduate years, Tim Alberta engaged himself in the study of journalism, taking up the knowledge of seasoned teachers and connecting with other students who shared his love for narrative and truth-seeking.

He polished his expertise as a writer, diving into the complexities of reporting and having a sharp eye for detail.

Tim's attention to his studies and his unshakable commitment to greatness garnered him distinction as an outstanding student, laying the scene for his future success in the profession of journalism.

Outside of the classroom, Tim Alberta looked for chances to obtain practical experience in the field of media. He interned at local newspapers and media sites, eager to use his abilities in real-world situations and get firsthand experience in the sector. These early experiences gave him crucial insights into the inner workings of newsrooms and reinforced his enthusiasm for investigative reporting and storytelling.

Throughout his formative years, Tim Alberta's background, schooling, and early interests merged to establish the cornerstone of his career in political journalism.

His persistent devotion to truth-seeking, his voracious curiosity about the world around him, and his natural ability for writing all lay the framework for his eventual success as a significant figure in American journalism.

As Tim Alberta's journey developed, it became evident that his upbringing and family history had infused him with a profound sense of purpose and an unshakable devotion to greatness. These formative years placed him on a course toward becoming one of the most regarded voices in political journalism, where he continues to make substantial contributions to the profession and affect the national discussion.

CHAPTER 2

RISE TO JOURNALISM

Tim Alberta's career in journalism begins with a deep-seated passion for stories and a dogged desire for truth. His early years in Michigan established the groundwork for his future career, as he polished his abilities as a writer and reporter and gained a keen interest in current events and politics.

After graduating from Michigan State University with a degree in journalism, Tim Alberta's career took off when he joined the National Review, a prominent conservative periodical noted for its keen political criticism and analysis. It was here that he began to develop a name for himself as a rising star in the world of political journalism.

At the National Review, Tim Alberta's flair for storytelling and his ability to give incisive insights on knotty political topics immediately caught the attention of readers and colleagues alike. His pieces were acclaimed for their depth of research, clarity of thought, and intriguing narrative style, winning him a loyal following and establishing his place as a powerful voice in the conservative media scene.

Tim Alberta's journey to stardom at the National Review was powered by his unrelenting attention to quality and his ability to integrate intricate political occurrences into simple, riveting prose. His reporting on key policy debates, election campaigns, and legislative challenges revealed his ability to unearth the human stories behind the headlines and put light on the inner workings of American politics.

As his reputation continued to rise at the National Review, Tim Alberta's particular blend of incisive critique and engaging storytelling set him out as a journalist to watch.

His work received global recognition and secured his standing as a key figure in political journalism, laying the path for the next phase in his career.

In 2014, Tim Alberta made a brave action that would further strengthen his status in the sphere of political journalism. He joined Politico, a prominent media firm recognized for its extensive coverage of national politics and its vital role in defining the political debate.

At Politico, Tim Alberta's journalistic talents found a new platform, enabling him to dig even further into the heart of American politics and give unique insights into the inner workings of Washington, D.C. His coverage of the 2016 presidential campaign was unusually significant, as he brought his normal blend of astute analysis and engaging storytelling to bear on one of the most consequential political events in recent memory.

Tim Alberta's reporting on the 2016 election thrilled readers and solidified his reputation as a top voice in political journalism. His in-depth profiles of significant political individuals, his sharp analysis of campaign strategies, and his ability to catch the pulse of the American voter set him apart as a journalist of extraordinary talent and insight.

Throughout his stint at Politico, Tim Alberta continued to establish himself as a journalist of extraordinary talent and ethics. His reporting on the complexities of American politics, his ability to cut through the noise and give clarity on vital matters, and his steadfast passion for truth-seeking gained him immense sympathy and respect from readers, colleagues, and industry peers.

Tim Alberta's beginnings in journalism were defined by an unwavering devotion to quality, a natural flair for storytelling, and an intense curiosity about the world around him. From his formative years in Michigan to his rise to prominence at the National Review and his impactful coverage of the 2016 election at Politico, he has consistently demonstrated a rare blend of journalistic prowess and intellectual depth that sets him apart as a true luminary in the field of political journalism.

As he continues to make important contributions to the national discussion and impact the future of American media, it is apparent that Tim Alberta's beginnings in journalism have created the framework for a remarkable career defined by ethics, intellect, and an unrelenting devotion to truth-seeking. His journey from Michigan to the national stage stands as a testimony to the power of storytelling, the quest for greatness, and the enduring influence of a writer determined to put a light on the complexity of our world.

CHAPTER 3

REPORTING APPROACH AND LIFESTYLE

Tim Alberta is a famous political reporter recognized for his in-depth coverage of the Republican Party and the conservative movement.

His unusual style and manner have allowed him to give important insights into key political persons and events, ultimately affecting the political discussion and media landscape.

Alberta's reporting approach is defined by its thoroughness and attention to detail. He is famous for going deep into the inner workings of the Republican Party, revealing the reasons and strategies of significant people within the conservative movement. His journalistic style is typified by a fair and objective tone, letting readers draw their judgments based on the material presented.

When it comes to coverage of the Republican Party, Alberta attempts to give a complete understanding of the party's dynamics, both at the national and local levels. He goes beyond the surface-level examination, attempting to comprehend the basic factors that drive the party's decision-making processes. His journalism often sheds light on the internal rivalries and power battles within the party, offering readers a detailed insight into its inner workings.

In addition to his coverage of the Republican Party, Alberta's work also extends to the conservative movement as a whole. He aims to understand the philosophical underpinnings of conservatism and how they arise in today's political arena. By presenting insights into the numerous organizations within the conservative movement, Alberta gives a diversified picture of this key political force.

Alberta's reporting is distinguished by his ability to obtain access to critical political personalities and events. He has gained a reputation for conducting in-depth interviews with important politicians, bringing readers fresh insights into their thinking and goals. His reporting generally contains behind-the-scenes accounts of significant political events, allowing readers an intimate glance into the decision-making processes that shape our nation's politics.

One of Alberta's abilities is his ability to humanize political people, showing them as multifaceted persons with their own personal and professional struggles. This method encourages readers to look behind the public personas of these leaders, acquiring a greater comprehension of their actions and intentions. By humanizing these folks, Alberta adds depth and complexity to his reporting, giving a more fascinating and relevant tale for his viewers.

Alberta's reporting has had a major effect on the political discussion and media environment. His in-depth research has provided readers with a broader awareness of the Republican Party and conservative movement, questioning traditional views and giving new perspectives.

By putting light on the fundamental workings of these political dynamics, Alberta has aided in promoting a more informed and nuanced public discourse.

Furthermore, Alberta's reporting has altered the media landscape by creating a high standard for political journalism. His hard research and fair reporting style have set an example for aspiring journalists, underlining the necessity for honesty and impartiality in political reporting.

By upholding these principles, Alberta has upped the bar for political journalism, encouraging others to follow suit in their reporting.

Tim Alberta's political reporting process and style are defined by their thoroughness, impartiality, and insightfulness. His coverage of the Republican Party and conservative movement goes beyond surface-level analysis, allowing readers a deeper knowledge of these key political forces. Through his in-depth interviews and behind-the-scenes accounts, Alberta gives unique insights into key political persons and events, ultimately shaping the political discourse and media landscape.

CHAPTER 4

NOTABLE INTERVIEWS AND COVERAGE

Tim Alberta's remarkable interviews and reportage have been a cornerstone of his career as a political journalist. His ability to arrange open and informative interviews with important leaders inside the Republican Party has set him apart as a recognized and respected voice in the world of political reporting.

One of Alberta's most memorable interviews was with former President Donald Trump. In this rare and wide-ranging talk, Alberta looked into Trump's political approach, personal motives, and the factors that have created his leadership. The interview provides vital insights into Trump's leadership style and decision-making process, providing light on the inner workings of the Trump administration.

Alberta's interview with Senate Majority Leader Mitch McConnell was another great milestone in his career.

McConnell, famed for his political brilliance and influence inside the Republican Party, provided Alberta an honest glimpse into the dynamics of power within the Senate and the problems of governing a highly divided party. The conversation gave vital insights into McConnell's approach to government and his vision for the future of the GOP.

In addition to his high-profile interviews with political leaders, Alberta has also done in-depth chats with grassroots activists, party operatives, and significant contributors. These interviews have enabled him to record the opinions of people who are generally neglected in popular political coverage, offering a more thorough and nuanced insight into the dynamics at play inside the Republican Party.

Alberta's coverage of significant events and changes inside the Republican Party has been similarly noteworthy.

From national conventions to critical legislative fights, Alberta has been on the front lines of political reporting, delivering insightful analysis and on-the-ground insights into the inner workings of the GOP.

One of Alberta's most noteworthy moments in political journalism was his coverage of the 2016 presidential election. Alberta's reporting provides a deep dive into the mechanics of the Republican primary contest, allowing readers a behind-the-scenes look at the plans, rivalries, and alliances that affected the result of the election. His reportage shed light on the growth of Donald Trump as a political force and the fissures within the Republican Party that prepared the path for his win.

Alberta's work on the 2020 election cycle was equally profound, presenting readers with a full picture of the dynamics at play in defining the future of the Republican Party. From the development of populist groups to the influence of demographic changes on electoral strategy, Alberta's coverage presented a rich tapestry of insights into the developing dynamics of American politics.

In addition to his work on national politics, Alberta has also covered state and local campaigns, offering readers a greater knowledge of the grassroots movements and regional dynamics that impact the wider political scene. His reportage has emphasized the range of opinions and interests inside the Republican Party, presenting a more nuanced depiction of its internal dynamics.

Alberta's ability to interact with a broad variety of sources and convey their opinions has been a trademark of his reporting. Whether interviewing government leaders, party insiders, or regular residents, Alberta has shown a great ability to obtain frank and enlightening insights that deepen his reporting and offer readers a more thorough grasp of the topics at hand.

Overall, Tim Alberta's remarkable interviews and reportage have positioned him as a major voice in political journalism. His ability to arrange insightful conversations with important players and give sharp analysis of political events has made him a valued source for those trying to grasp the complexity of American politics. Alberta's devotion to extensive research, impartial reporting, and empathic storytelling has set him apart as a journalist who provides depth and insight to his coverage of the Republican Party and beyond.

CHAPTER 5

PERSONAL LIFE AND RELATIONSHIPS

Tim Alberta is a political journalist and author recognized for his insightful reporting and in-depth conversations with important people inside the Republican Party. However, despite his professional triumphs, there is a human aspect to Tim Alberta that is equally captivating.

Born and reared in Michigan, Tim Alberta's background has had a key part in defining his views and ideals. Growing up in a middle-class household, he learned the significance of hard work, tenacity, and ethics from an early age. These basic beliefs have been obvious in his approach to journalism and his dedication to producing impartial and informative reporting.

Tim Alberta's personal life is distinguished by a strong feeling of family and community. He has frequently talked about the impact of his parents, who instilled in him a great sense of understanding and compassion for others.

Their support and assistance have been crucial in forming his character and directing his career aspirations.

In addition to his family, Tim Alberta's personal life is strengthened by his ties with friends and coworkers.

Known for his pleasant attitude and genuine interest in people, he has developed lasting ties with folks from all backgrounds and walks of life. These interactions have not only enhanced his personal life but also supplied him with unique insights and viewpoints that have impacted his reporting.

Tim Alberta's personal life also includes a profound interest in books, music, and the arts. An avid reader with a high love for narrative, he has frequently acknowledged the works of writers such as F. Scott Fitzgerald, Ernest Hemingway, and Joan Didion as sources of inspiration. His music appreciation encompasses a broad spectrum of genres, from classical to rock, reflecting his varied tastes and open-minded attitude to cultural expression.

In his own time, Tim Alberta likes outdoor activities such as hiking, skiing, and exploring nature. His admiration for the natural world and the peace it brings acts as a contrast to the intensity of his professional activities. Whether enjoying a walk along a woodland route or tackling a tough mountain top, he finds serenity and refreshment in the great outdoors.

Tim Alberta's personal life is also distinguished by a strong sense of political participation and social responsibility. He has been actively engaged in community service efforts, devoting his time and talents to causes that are important to his heart. His passion to make a good influence on society reflects his strongly held conviction in the potential of human action to achieve significant change.

In terms of relationships, Tim Alberta's personal life comprises a close-knit band of friends and confidants whom he appreciates profoundly. Known for his commitment and steadfast support, he has formed lifelong ties with those who share his ideals and enthusiasm for making a difference in the world. These interactions serve as a source of strength and inspiration, giving him the encouragement and perspective, he needs to manage life's problems.

The focus of Tim Alberta's personal life is his family. A dedicated husband and father, he appreciates the time spent with his loved ones and takes great satisfaction in cultivating deep and meaningful ties with them. His job as a father has improved his knowledge of empathy, patience, and unconditional love, improving his own life in fundamental ways.

Tim Alberta's personal life is defined by a profound sense of purpose, compassion, and connection. His background, beliefs, hobbies, and relationships have all contributed to forming the varied man he is today. Whether digging into the nuances of political reporting or appreciating peaceful moments with loved ones, he tackles each element of his own life with deliberation, honesty, and an unshakable determination to have a good influence on the world around him.

CHAPTER 6

CHALLENGES AND VICTORIES

Tim Alberta is a prominent political writer and author noted for his astute analysis and in-depth reporting on the problems and successes of American politics. Throughout his career, Alberta has encountered various hurdles and disappointments but has finally emerged as one of the most recognized voices in the business. His story is a monument to endurance, determination, and the quest for truth in a continuously altering terrain.

One of the major problems Alberta has encountered in his career is the unrelenting strain of reporting on the volatile realm of American politics. As a journalist, he has been charged with negotiating the complicated web of political intrigue, ideological differences, and party battles that characterize the current political environment.

This has forced him to maintain a persistent dedication to honesty and integrity, even in the face of severe scrutiny and criticism.

In addition to the obvious problems of political reporting, Alberta has also met personal hurdles along the road. The responsibilities of his career have frequently compelled him to sacrifice time with loved ones and neglect personal pleasures to make deadlines and pursue vital stories. The toll of this rigorous lifestyle has created its own set of obstacles for Alberta, but his steadfast passion for his art has allowed him to endure and continue creating high-quality work.

Despite these hurdles, Alberta has achieved significant wins over his career that have reinforced his status as a major voice in political journalism. His ability to identify and report on significant issues has garnered him great accolades and respect within the business. His work has thrown light on significant topics, kept powerful persons responsible, and offered essential insights into the inner workings of American politics.

Alberta's accomplishments extend beyond his reporting, as he has also found significant success as a novelist. His book "American Carnage: On the Front Lines of the Republican Civil War and the Rise of President Trump" earned considerable notice and critical praise for its penetrating examination of the Republican Party's internal strife and the elevation of Donald Trump to the presidency. The book confirmed Alberta's reputation as a top expert on American politics and further entrenched his legacy as a powerful journalist and novelist.

In addition to his professional triumphs, Alberta's ability to adapt to the continuously changing media world stands as another victory in his career. As conventional journalism has transformed in the digital age, Alberta has shown a remarkable aptitude to utilize new platforms and technology to reach bigger audiences and connect with readers in novel ways. His openness to accept change and seek new channels for narrative has enabled him to stay at the forefront of political journalism.

Throughout his career, Tim Alberta has negotiated a range of hurdles while attaining tremendous victories in the field of political journalism. His unrelenting devotion to truth, his ability to find major stories, and his readiness to adapt to change have reinforced his standing as a recognized and powerful personality in American journalism. As he continues to confront new problems and chase revolutionary stories, it is obvious that Alberta's legacy will survive as a monument to the lasting power of devoted journalism in altering our knowledge of politics and society.

CHAPTER 7

Tim Alberta is a renowned personality in the field of political journalism, noted for his effective reporting and astute analysis. His impact goes well beyond the pages of the newspapers he works for, as he has become a trusted voice in the sphere of American politics.

As a journalist, Tim Alberta has had a tremendous influence on the way political events are reported and perceived by the public. His work is marked by its depth and subtlety, as he dives into complicated subjects with a strong eye for detail and a devotion to presenting the complete picture. This attention to detailed and intelligent reporting has won him a reputation as a journalist of honesty and intelligence.

One of the primary ways in which Tim Alberta has made his impact on the realm of political journalism is through his ability to give insight and commentary that goes beyond the headlines. In a day of rapid-fire news cycles and sensationalized reporting, Alberta's methodical and analytical approach stands out. His writing is defined by its depth and complexity, as he attempts to offer his readers a thorough grasp of the subjects at hand.

Alberta's impact goes beyond the written word, as he is also a sought-after pundit and analyst. His appearances on television and radio have enabled him to reach a broader audience and give his views on the current scene. His observations are respected not merely for their accuracy and depth but also for their ability to cut through the noise and bring clarity in a complicated and sometimes perplexing environment.

In addition to his work in conventional media, Tim Alberta has also embraced new modes of communication to spread his reach even further. His active presence on social media platforms enables him to communicate directly with his audience, expressing his views and observations in real time. This direct connection has allowed him to create a devoted following and further consolidate his status as a trusted voice in the world of political journalism.

Alberta's effect and influence are also visible in the way his work has affected public conversation and understanding of critical political problems. His reporting has cast light on major topics and events, offering a crucial service to the public by informing and educating them about the workings of government and the forces that define our political environment.

Furthermore, Alberta's impact may be observed in the way his work has resonated with other journalists and pundits. His careful approach and devotion to truth have set a high bar for others in the sector, motivating them to strive for excellence in their reporting. In this sense, Alberta's impact goes beyond his work, affecting the larger landscape of political journalism.

Tim Alberta's effect and influence on the field of political journalism are unquestionable. Through his astute reporting, intelligent analysis, and entertaining commentary, he has become a trusted voice in American politics. His work has not only enlightened and educated the public, but has also established a high bar for journalistic quality. As he continues to make his imprint on the field, it is apparent that his impact will only continue to expand.

CHAPTER 8

KEY LESSONS

1. Stay loyal to your ideals and principles, even when it's tough or controversial.

2. Dedicate yourself to your trade and continually seek to better yourself.

3. Don't be hesitant to ask challenging questions and hold powerful individuals responsible.

4. Be willing to take chances and venture out of your comfort zone.

5. Embrace failure as a learning opportunity and utilize it to drive your progress.

6. Build solid ties with mentors, coworkers, and sources.

7. Be persistent and tenacious in pursuing your objectives.

8. Stay educated and up-to-date on current events and trends. 37

9. Use your platform to elevate the voices of underrepresented people and promote social justice.

10. Believe in the power of narrative to impact change and inspire others.

CHAPTER 9

TRANSFORMATIVE
EXERCISES

1. What beliefs and concepts do I hold most dear, and how have they informed my job choices?

____

____

____

____

____

____

____

____

2. How have I devoted myself to enhancing my skills, and what actions can I take to continue progressing in my field?

____

____

____

____

3. Have I been ready to raise challenging questions and hold strong individuals responsible in my profession, or have I run away from controversy?

____

____

____

____

4. In what instances have I moved out of my comfort zone to take chances and explore new opportunities?

____

____

____

____

5. How have I reacted to failure in the past, and what lessons have I gained from those experiences?

____

____

____

____

6. Have I created solid ties with mentors, coworkers, and sources, or do I like to operate independently?

____

____

____

____

____

7. How persistent and tenacious am I when it comes to pursuing my objectives, and what barriers have I overcome to attain success?

____

____

____

____

____

8. Do I keep educated and up-to-date on current events and trends in my profession, or do I depend on obsolete information and assumptions?

____

____

____

____

9. How have I utilized my position to promote social justice and elevate the voices of oppressed communities?

____

____

____

____

10. Do I believe in the power of narrative to influence change, and how can I harness that potential in my work?

CONCLUSION

Tim Alberta has gone a long way from his modest origins in Brighton, Michigan, where he dreamt of becoming a baseball writer. He has experienced and recorded some of the most crucial periods in American politics, from the rise and collapse of the Tea Party to the election and administration of Donald Trump. He has developed a reputation as one of the most analytical and authoritative journalists of his time, with a flair for portraying the intricacies and complexity of the ideological conflict between and between the two parties. He has also published a best-selling book, American Carnage, that presents a complete and riveting narrative of the Republican Civil War and the development of Trumpism.

In his path, Tim Alberta has experienced numerous problems and chances. He has worked for numerous major magazines, such as National Review, National Journal, The Wall Street Journal, POLITICO, and The Atlantic. He has moderated a Democratic primary debate, interviewed famous politicians and activists, and featured as a pundit on various television shows. He has also relocated back to his home state of Michigan, where he has concentrated on chronicling the tales and feelings of regular Americans, particularly those who have been touched by the epidemic, the economic crisis, the racial turmoil, and the political division.

Through his writing, Tim Alberta has not only educated and enlightened his readers but also inspired and challenged them. He has highlighted the necessity of journalism as a public service, a civic responsibility, and a moral imperative. He has exhibited the benefits of inquiry, ethics, and empathy in his work. He has also highlighted the variety, dynamism, and resilience of the American people, as well as the fragility, uncertainty, and possibility of American democracy.

Tim Alberta is more than simply a journalist. He is a storyteller, a historian, a critic, and a witness. He is a voice of reason, a force of truth, and a catalyst for change. He is a biographer of his nation, his party, and his period. He is an outstanding person, whose life and accomplishments ought to be acknowledged and admired.